Happy Healthy
For Dogs

A Handbook for All Stages of Your Pet's Life

Contents

Introduction - Pages 2 - 8

Nutrition: The Science Behind All That Noise - Pages 9 - 24

The Best Exercise for Your Dog - Pages 25 - 38

Supplements - Pages - 39 - 59

Husbandry and Grooming: How to Pamper Your Dog - Pages 60 - 72

Safety: Protect Your Dog from Hazards You May Overlook - Pages - 73 - 83

How to Train Your Dog - Pages 84 - 107

Detect Illness: How to Catch Chronic Problems Early - Pages 108 - 128

Trends to Avoid - Pages - 129 - 137

The Golden Years: Taking Care of Your Aging Dog - Pages - 138 - 148

Saying Goodbye - Pages 149 - 161

Some Final Notes - Pages 162 - 168

Chapter 1

A dog is a valuable family member who energizes you, returns your love a thousandfold, and brings immense joy to your days. Studies have found that dog parents are healthier and happier. Dogs reduce your risk for heart disease, improve your response to stress, and help you live longer. Dogs keep you active, and yes, science shows that your dog makes you appear more attractive to other people. What's not to love about dogs? A healthy, happy dog can bring you and your family a tremendous amount of joy.

Sadly, it can be all too easy for this joy to be overshadowed

"Dogs are not our whole life, but they make our lives whole." Animal welfare advocate Roger A. Caras

by preventable issues. The hardest things to deal with are the unknowns, the risks that you're not even aware of. This book covers everything you could think of and beyond. You can be sure that this is a guide that contains all the information you need to be the best parent for your pet.

Eliminate the Guesswork

Say good-bye to Google rabbit holes and frantically sifting through hundreds of conflicting opinions as you try to find the facts. Whenever you face a challenge, you can turn to a chapter in this guide. To prepare for a new dog, or to deal with a new phase in an old friend's life, you can always find advice in the guide.

This book is for you whether you're a first-time dog owner or a seasoned caretaker of your best friend. Written with extensive consultation from Taryn Arsenault, a lifetime dog owner who worked as a vet tech and veterinary hospital manager, this book is designed to help you with any question you have about being a good parent to your dog. Every dog owner's situation is unique; therefore, these lessons are general guidelines – not rules – that may be adapted by careful research to meet your current needs. This book will help you find the right questions to ask your vet. It will help you assess all the situations where you need to involve your vet, all while limiting preventable, emergency visits. When you limit the chances of emergencies and preventable treatments, you and your vet can focus on giving your dog its best life. This book will guide you about all the questions your vet can answer and all the ways you can make your pet's life better and longer.

From the early years of the puppy stage to the hard questions of senior and end-of-life care, we've got you covered.

Learn How to Make Informed Choices

We cut through all the noise of companies and the (very, very few) vets who want to make money off your love and concern for your pet. We'll help you get to vets who are genuinely concerned about your dog's wellbeing.

This guide will provide you tools to do your own research, so that you can be certain you have the right veterinarian, the right information.

> "After years of having a dog, you know him. You know the meaning of his snuffs and grunts and barks. Every twitch of the ears is a question or statement, every wag of the tail is an exclamation."
> Novelist Robert McCammon

In our guides about how to care for your dog, we will empower you with strategies to make **your own informed decisions** for the best quality of life for your pet.

Strengthen Your Collaboration with Your Vet

Remember, nothing can come close to the level of expertise a veterinarian has. A veterinarian has gone through at least 8 years of higher education, 8 years of studying animals, and that makes them the most qualified to take care of your dog.

The problem with veterinary care is that vets have patients that cannot talk to them. That's why it's so important that you're informed and alert. We'll tell you all you need to look out for and all the right questions to make sure you help your vet understand your dog and treat them as effectively as possible.

Comprising short, comprehensive chapters, this book will help you navigate everything you need to know about nutrition, supplements, safety, training... you name it. From Taryn, a veterinarian clinic/hospital manager, as well as a long-time pet owner, comes the expertise and experience needed to give the best possible advice. In the next 11 chapters, we will be your friends and we'll give you the answers, and most importantly, the tools to reach your **own** answers for the best life experience for **your** dog.

Chapter 2

Nutrition: The Science Behind All That Noise

You must have a lot of questions about what food is best for your dog. Should you just get dog food from the grocery store? Dry or wet food? Carnivore or omnivore? Canine nutrition, like human nutrition, is a science. Let us guide you in this chapter about the best practices of making sure your dog is not only fed, however, also thriving and beautiful

Passersby stop Taryn's family all the time when they walk Jasper. He's an almost-year-old German Short-haired Pointer mixed with Labrador Retriever. He's a large dog, already at almost 85 lb., pure black, with just a bit of white. With a gorgeous, shiny coat,

> "Pets are humanizing. They remind us we have an obligation and responsibility to preserve and nurture and care for all life." James Cromwell

Jasper attracts a lot of loving attention.

The question people have is, "How did his coat get so shiny?" You can find the best dog breed as a pet. However, a mediocre diet will show in your dog's health and appearance. This is why a close eye on nutrients is important.

Know Your Breed

It is important to be breed specific. Jasper is a large breed dog whose family have to be aware of his joints and his hips. Some labs are prone to skin issues.

Focus on knowing your breed and what the dog needs to ensure a healthy and balanced diet. Some breeds are more prone to specific issues. Keeping track of the issues will help you tailor your diet for your dog.

Joint Issues

Newfoundlands, Rottweilers, Golden and Labrador Retrievers, Basset Hounds, Saint Bernards and Cocker Spaniels often have serious joint issues.

Thyroid Issues

Many breeds of dogs are susceptible to hypothyroidism, especially as they age. Cocker spaniels. Rottweilers and German Shepherds are some of these breeds.

Eyesight

Bulldogs, due to being overbred, are especially susceptible.

How to choose the best quality of food

Choosing dog food should be no small matter. Taryn spent three full days choosing food for her dog Jasper. With advice from your vet and your own vigilance, make sure your pet only has the best. Here are some tips to make sure you're on the right track:

- Look at your nutritional label. What is the very first thing? If it is not meat, it's not high quality. If it's chicken meal or beef meal, that's not enough. Is it chicken? Is it duck meat? Is it beef or whatever meat you feed your pet? That needs to be the very first thing listed in the ingredients, then you know right off the bat that you're starting with quality food. You'll know that it is not a byproduct-based food, rather it is a whole food.

- Ingredients that are low in the list can also harm your dog. Some dogs would not even have a hint of stomach upset if they ate a tire. But there are dogs like Jasper, who has a peanut allergy. Aside from allergens, check for filler ingredients. Lower quality pet food often has fillers that are not exactly harmful, but affect the nutrient density of the food.
- Don't forget to check reviews for dog food. Scour the internet for reputable sources of honest reviews. Look for the common factors in positive and negative reviews. Maybe most of the negative reviews are by people who have a specific breed of dog that reacted poorly to an ingredient.
- Research the company that makes the food. Many companies that produce pet food have faced issues in the past with recalls due to contamination. Some have been exposed for misleading advertising and making claims about

ingredients and quality that were discovered to be false. Make sure the company is compliant with government regulations.

What's Wrong With Grocery Store Pet Food?

No, getting pet food should not be as easy as throwing in a few cans while you buy your own groceries. This may seem like an extreme opinion to some people. Of course, pet food from the grocery store will not instantly kill your pet. However, you will notice that lack of nutrition will take its toll as your pet ages, and shows signs of chronic issues.

Grocery store food is generally mass-produced, so the quality of ingredients is low. These include lots of preservatives, fillers, and lower quality meats. Better quality food costs more for a reason. High-end food producers make the effort to choose good cuts of meat, add extra amino acids and more bioavailable nutrients.

Think about your budget and your own ideal diet. You know the difference between canned lunch meat and a New York strip. You strike a balance between luxurious food and cheaper options. In the same way, you can get moderately priced, high quality food for your dog without breaking the bank.

Be careful about fads

This is the other side of the coin when it comes to dog diet. While some people just buy pet food from their grocery store, others can fall prey to trends in search of the best of the best.

Diets

Don't be lulled into the thought of a raw food diet being the best thing, or only a solid protein or a wheat free type diet. If your dog does not show any types of issues with corn or wheat as a carb mixed into their dog food, don't worry about it. Dogs absolutely need a balanced diet just like a human, they need all the food groups. There's a lot of pet store brand foods now that try to tell you, or make you think, that by giving them a gluten free diet, somehow, you're doing something better for them. It's an absolute fallacy, unless your dog has shown to have a specific allergy to that grain.[1]

Dog Food Companies

Research the company that is making the food, make sure that they have not had any recalls on food or is being cited for false nutritional values. A couple of years ago, a very large company was nailed and fined US$7 million for mislabeling their dog food. Their food did not contain all the wonderful things they claimed it had. Instead of the full ingredients claimed on the packaging, they used cheap by-products.2

Find a good vet

A caring, concerned veterinarian is a valuable resource in finding the proper food. Put as much time and effort as you can in finding a good vet. Then do your own research, by looking at scientific studies or clinical trials and make sure the trials are not funded by a pet food manufacturer. Your best asset is a vet who'll give you an unbiased opinion about your dog's diet.

The different stages

As your dog grows, its nutrition needs to change. You can't pick a canine food brand on the day you get a new puppy and feed it to your new friend every day for years to come.

In the puppy stage, it's extremely important to ensure a high-quality diet. In these early stages of development, an inadequate diet will lead to non-stop health issues. For the sake of your dog's long-term well-being, pay special attention to the puppy's needs.

Puppies

Puppies, especially large breeds, need **high protein diets**. It is imperative to their long-term health, as if they do not get enough protein in the early stages of development, then you will have continuous health issues.

Taryn's family were worried about Jasper's health because of his large size. They ensured from the get-go that his diet was incredibly high in omega three fatty acids, glucosamine, and chondroitin, along with other fish oils that are known to help for healthy joints and healthy skin. There are secrets to a shiny, healthy coat. The dog's inner health will show on its skin and hair.

As a dog enters their first year, you should be transitioning into a more moderated diet. You should still focus heavily on protein, but also start looking at the long-term.

Balance it with fresh fruits and veggies keeping in mind to do your research as to which ones are beneficial for the breed and age of your dog, as some fruits and vegetables are poisonous for your dog, along with keeping a very close eye on omega 3s.

Mid-life

At 2-7 years of age, your dog's nutrition needs change like you'd expect your own needs to change, you are now basically keeping a closer eye on caloric intake, because a lot of dogs as they age have the same issues we do, namely, you don't need as many carbs in your 40s as you did in your 20s.

Now, you are more balanced in your pet's diet. Meals are less frequent, but nutrient-dense.

As we ourselves age, we focus on foods that bring down inflammation. We focus on foods that help our joints stay healthy, and focus on foods that are good for your heart, or our digestive system, and in the same way you are now looking for foods that are going to help your dog have a nice, balanced diet.

7 years to end of life

What should you feed an aging dog? This is always an interesting question, because so many people feel, "my dog is a senior, I'm just gonna let it live its life and not worry about its diet."

This can cause so many unnecessary health issues and cause a lot of discomfort for the dog. It will cause unnecessary visits to the vet and expensive treatment to help your dog with pain management. There's a reason why specialized senior care and diet exists.

A senior pet can average four to five years. This is dependent upon the help of a balanced diet for their age and condition.

Extend Your Dog's Life

Taryn's family has a senior dog, a Kelpie. She's completely blind, and she has a thyroid condition. However, she is quite happy, despite her elderly issues. She eats a proper diet. She gets supplements because of her thyroid issues, and this helps her skin and coat. She has lived 3 years past her life expectancy as a happy, healthy dog.

Just because your dog has turned seven, it doesn't mean that suddenly you pull away nutrition and say the sky's the limit. You wouldn't do that to your 50- or 60-year-old parents. You encourage them to stay healthy. It's the same with your senior animal because the healthier you keep them, the better and the longer you'll have them as a pet, a happy healthy friend.

Key Takeaways:

- A balanced, nutritious diet is the secret to a glowing, active, problem-free dog.
- Know your breed. Some breeds are more prone to certain conditions that a good diet can help prevent.
- A small dog's needs will be different from a larger dog's
- Beware of fad diets and fast-talking vets. Do your research.
- At different life stages, your dog's nutrition needs will change.
- A good diet will keep your dog happy and healthy well into their senior years, while helping you cut your vet bills in half

Chapter 3
The Best Exercise for Your Dog

How important is exercise for my dog? Should I take my dog on longer walks? What other kinds of exercise are there?

Exercise is key for all aspects of your dog's health including its physical and mental health as well as emotional well-being. As trainer Sarah Pennington says, **"A healthy dog is a happy dog."** You don't really realize how important it is until you remove the access to exercise.

When Taryn's dog Jasper was about six or seven months old, everybody in the house came down with a cold. He wasn't getting his daily walks, his playtime in the backyard, or his training sessions, because everybody was sick. Fast forward a couple of days, everybody started to feel better, so they had to go out and do some

"Never stand between a dog and the fire hydrant."— John Peer

groceries. They came home to a destroyed $800 leather sofa and a brand new $200 hand-woven bamboo blinds in pieces. He was just frenetic. He had not been exercised or mentally stimulated enough within the last couple days and out of that lack of needed activity, he literally destroyed the living room.

Know Your Breed

We keep repeating this for a reason. Not every dog will react like Jasper did from a lack of physical exercise. He's a **pointer dog**, who not only needs physical exercise, he needs mental stimulation as well. His breed of dogs is bred to hunt, which is a workout for the body and the brain. You could take him out on a 10km run and get his physical workout, but he'd still be bored at the end of the day if he does not get a mental workout included.

You can't generalize based on size. It's true that most small dogs, like Chihuahuas, need only 20-30 minutes of exercise a day. However, toy poodles, for example, are a very intelligent breed and need more. They need longer walks for their minds.

Sight hounds like greyhounds and whippets are runners and explorers, but they don't need a lot of exercise. Two 20-minute sprints, and then they'll sleep all day. They also like to explore areas on their own, so keep in mind that you need to have access to fenced yards or gardens.

Giant breeds don't need much exercise. You may think a Great Dane needs a lot of exercise, but these dogs and other giant ones like Saint Bernards and Leonbergers only need short, moderate paced walks. These dogs are big. They have huge frames that only require some movement for healthy joints. However, they also don't need too much because moving their body requires a lot of energy.

Herding Dogs like collie breeds and corgis are happiest when they know what their job is in a household. They need mental and physical exercise. See our upcoming section on agility training.

On the other hand, there are dogs with great exercise needs, even up to 2 hours a day.

- Sporting breeds, like Retrievers, Springer Spaniels, and Poodles
- Working breeds, such as Dobermans, Huskies and Rottweilers.
- Herding breeds, like Sheepdogs, Collies and Shepherds

Keep in mind also that brachycephalic dog breeds, who have faces that are squashed in, like pugs, only need 20-30 minutes. They often have problems due to their facial structure and can overheat.

Scent hounds and terriers, like beagles, basset hounds and westies do well with 60–90-minute walks.

Exercise & Walking

Exercise includes many kinds of engagement with your dog's body, mind, and emotions. Many dog breeds will do great with just moderate walks, but you need to be aware of their needs.

Agility Training

What is agility training? Agility training is tailored to specific breeds of dogs. Their breed is meant to move quickly in multiple, tiered levels so that they are challenged.2

Herding dogs love agility training for mental stimulation. They'll have fun running up and down ramps and jumping over hurdles.

Swimming

Giant dogs love to swim! They enjoy it and need it. The water keeps pressure off their joints while allowing them to maintain their mobility through the years.

Giant dogs are too heavy for agility training. They're all bone and muscles and may even be harmed if you try to train them for agility. Swimming is the perfect exercise for them.

Mental Stimulation

Your unique pet, as per its personality and breed needs a tailored approach to mental stimulation. You could walk your dog for many miles a day, but still find it tearing apart your couch in search of a mental challenge. Many activities are mentally stimulating for dogs, depending on their preference.

Snuggles

Yes, they count! For all dogs, snuggles are a form of emotional and mental stimulation. For some small dogs, snuggles are all the mental stimulation they need in a day. Your hunting breed, however, will want more than that.

Sniffing During Walks

Please don't yank at your dog! Let it sniff the fire hydrant for more than five seconds! Do you know why your dog sniffs the street? Dogs are ruled by their nose, and when they smell that fire hydrant, they see what all the other local dogs have to say. Maybe it's gross and we think it's disgusting. However, we're humans and they're dogs. They don't think it's gross.

Sniffing is essential for your dog's mental health. A study in 2019 shows that dogs who were allowed to freely sniff were more 'optimistic'! Moreover, when your dog reaches to sniff other dogs' rear-ends, it's taking part in a canine ritual that helps it make friends. Your dog is less likely to have behavior problems if it's allowed to have mental stimulation. Remember that sniffing is one of its most primal urges. It's important to let your best friend be its full self!

Exploring

Especially if you have a sight hound, let your dog explore. Let them roll in grass, let them discover new things on their own. You may be tired and are only trying to do your best when you hurry your dog along during its walk. Remember, walk time is all about your dog. Let them enjoy and explore to get their mental exercise.

Toys

High quality dog toys are worth it. These toys are amazing for mental stimulation for dogs such as ones that they must work at to get their treats. Trust us that you will want one for your dog. They may seem expensive, nevertheless, you will want to invest in it even for small dogs.

The great thing about toys is that they often have challenges built into them that give your dog a sense of purpose. If your dog spends most of the day at home alone, a toy gives it a goal to fulfill and keeps it occupied. Dogs are surprisingly just like us. We kill time with video games, board games, and social media. Dogs are intelligent. Toys let them use their intelligence and add purpose to their days.

Giving your dog a toy also gives you a break, especially if you're working from home. Dogs always want something to do, and you can't interact with them all the time. During your work meetings, or even when you just want to read peacefully, it's great to have toys. For example, there are balls that you fill up with kibbles, and your dog has to take the kibble out. That keeps them busy, and out of your way. Investing in toys is a good idea to give yourself a break.

Choose the Right Pet

Exercise is integral for an animal's well-being. Dogs, whether as house pets or bred to work, innately need to exercise. It not only keeps them healthy, but it also keeps them happy. If your dog is unhappy or showing other types of behavioral problems, then it is probably not getting exercise. In our experience, literally 70 to 80% of the time, a problem dog is just not getting enough exercise, be it physical, mental, or emotional.

Dogs need attention and interaction. They need a robust, tailored exercise regimen. Before you choose a pet or dog breed, be honest with yourself about how much time you have. If you don't have time for a dog who needs a daily 20-minute walk, there is no shame in getting a goldfish.

Key Takeaways:
- Consider the needs of your dog's breed for physical and mental stimulation.
- Modify your walks for your dog's needs.
- Introduce agility training or swimming- walks are not the only form of exercise!
- Your dog needs mental stimulation and interaction.
- Invest in toys to give yourself a break.
- Only get a dog you're ready for.

Chapter 4

Supplements

Do dogs need supplements too? Isn't a high-quality diet enough? What supplements should I give my dog?

When a dog is added to your home, you need to know what the dog's specific dietary needs are and be prepared to meet them as a responsible pet owner. It will ensure that the pet is getting the best care possible and will keep you out of the vet's office a lot more. This way, you can make sure that your animal is living a quality life.

Part of being a good pet owner is knowing what your breed of dog

"Money can buy you a fine dog, but only love can make him wag his tail." -Kinky Friedman

specifically needs and then meeting those needs. Like any other person in your family, an animal has specific needs. In your own family, not everyone always eats the same diet. Your kids or spouse may have specific dietary needs and you work to meet those needs. Read on to learn more about supplements and whether they're the right choice for your dog.

The Effect of a Poor Diet Lasts for Years

You may remember Taryn's senior dog, Lady. As a dog who continues to outlive her life expectancy as a happy pet, Lady has benefited greatly from supplements.

"15 years ago, Lady showed up at our parents' home. She was skinny, covered in grease and skinny as a rail. No one had any idea where she came from.

After a vain search for her owners, we decided to adopt this sweet, already trained dog. She had arrived at a perfect time for our family too: right after we had to put our lab down.

Sadly, it was clear that Lady's previous owners had neglected to provide her with a good diet. We took her to the vet to make sure everything was ok; however, we suspect that many of Lady's current issues are due to a poor diet in her early years.

Lady has severe hypothyroidism. This condition is very common in dogs, but a good diet since day one can keep it from progressing to an extreme case. Lady is also completely blind, another condition that a nutritious diet can help prevent. She is a happy dog with a healthy appetite, but her issues are unnecessary, preventable discomforts."

Does Your Dog Need Supplements?

Here are a few questions to ask yourself and figure out if supplements are right for your dog. If you have a tiny toy breed pet who lives its life on a couch, you probably don't need to worry about supplements till mid to senior life.

Is your dog adopted?

An adopted dog needs supplements to make up for possible neglect in its early years.

If you adopted your dog, even as a year-old puppy, you may know nothing about how it was fed before coming into your care. Neglect in early years can lead to problems later in life, just like Lady's extreme hypothyroidism.

How active is your dog?

Support animals with physically demanding tasks need high-quality supplements. Taryn's working dog, Jasper, has an incredibly busy life. Jasper is being trained currently to help Taryn's daughter. She has a hard time standing from a sitting position on the floor, due to her health issues. He is being trained to help her get up and she's 135 pounds. That's a lot of work for a therapy animal.

He's eating high quality food to support his large frame already. And even though he's only a year old, he is being given supplements to protect his joints. Taryn is making sure that he is being very well cared for, so that he can do his job and remain healthy for life.

If you have an athletic dog that is training for something, then you should be supplementing that dog because they're going to need extra, more than just the food. Even a very high-quality diet provides just the baseline of your dog's nutritional needs.

The media wants you to think that the food fits every need. However, it's a median baseline based on research from a variety of dogs. Specifically, if you have an active, working breed, you should be thinking about supplements. Supplements will support a busy dog's day to day activity and take care of its long-term needs.

How old is your dog?

During midlife and senior years, dogs can begin to show health issues that are typical for their breed. We don't ever want to say it's too late. Generally, it's better to start supplementing for potential issues as early as possible because prevention will save you many troubles. When you already see the problem, it's harder to control.

For active and large dogs, supplementing should begin in the first year of their life.
For small and less busy dogs, know your dog's breed and start supplementing during ages 2 to 7 years.

Focus Areas for Supplementation

There is so much disparity in the information available for supplementing. Even by vets. It's largely dependent on location as well. Talk to a veterinarian in the southeastern United States and they're going to tell you that puppy food from the local grocery store is just fine, you need not worry about anything. Or you can go to South Florida, where most dogs are very expensive, high end, premium bred. The veterinarian is not going to let you walk out of that office until your bill is at least $2,000 and you end up with an arm full of who knows what.

There's a huge disparity and again it comes down to what we believe in: Do your own research, know the breed of your dog, and understand your dog's day to day needs.

Taryn points out 3 areas to focus on when supplementing: oral care, joint care, and skincare. These are the three big ones.

Supplements for Oral Care

Natural remedies like Apple Cider Vinegar are recommended for issues like bad breath etc., but for long term health of the teeth and gums, these ingredients are crucial:

- Vitamin C
- Vitamin B-Complex

These are water soluble nutrients. They are not stored in your dog's body, so supplementation is a good strategy to make sure they have enough for their oral health.

Supplements for Joint Care

Don't wait until you see a problem. It's always better late than never, but if you're already seeing a problem, it can be difficult to control. Like us, dogs are at risk for arthritis and other issues.

For large, heavy dogs, joint care is important from the first year. Look for supplements containing these ingredients:

- Glucosamine
- Chondroitin

Glucosamine, a compound of glucose and glutamine, helps form cartilage in the joints. It's literally a building block of one of the most important parts of your dog's skeletal system.

Supplements for Skincare

No genetic advantages can beat a dog coat that shines from great health. The dog-owners you stop in the street use supplements to keep their dogs looking shiny and healthy. Look for these ingredients:

- Fish Oil
- Omega 3 Fatty Acids

Fish oil contains omega 3 fatty acids that not only make your dog look great, but also reduce inflammation and keep their joints healthy.

How to choose a supplement:

When you look for supplements, you want to find the ones that fulfill the following criteria:

- Easy to take for your dog. The best supplement is one you'll use everyday
- Made of high-quality ingredients. Nutrients come from many sources, but the best are ones that come from whole food sources
- Fun for your dog. A bonus to the point about ease. Good flavors that your dog looks forward to will make it easy and even enjoyable to add supplements.
- Research. The best brands prove their efficacy through clinical trials that support their claims.

To simplify your search for the best products for your dog, we're including a list of Elsantis supplements. When we couldn't find our perfect supplements, we worked with experts to create these, that fully align with what we want from high quality supplements. These are not your old pills. These are strips that dissolve in your dog's mouth so that the process is stress-free for us and our pets. They also come in great flavors, so that supplement time is something our dogs look forward to. No matter what brand of supplements you get, please make sure they fulfill all the requirements we listed. Here is a sample of our offerings:

- For anti-inflammatory effects and long-term health

Smoked Salmon flavored strips with Curcumin 50 mg + Boswellia 50 mg + MSM 25 mg + chondroitin 25 mg

- Arthritis support

Roast chicken flavored Serratiopeptidase - 40000 IU + Astaxanthin strip 4 mg + Glucosamine 20 mg + Cissus 20 mg

- Skin and coat

Maple Syrup flavored Omega 3 60 mg + Biotin 5000 mcg + Folic acid 400 mcg + DHA 40 mg

- Calm

Turkey flavored Melatonin 0.6 mg + (Suntheanine) L-Theanine 40 mg + Chamomile - 20 mg + Tryptophan 20 mg

- Gut Health

Peanut butter flavored Probiotics Blend 5 Bill CFU cranberry extract 30mg

- Dental Health

Mint flavored Citrox-Bioflavinoids

No matter which company you buy from, your dog will benefit from supplements that are made of high quality ingredients, are well-researched, and are easy or even fun to take. A lower quality supplement will not have good bioavailability. At the very least, it will only make your dog's pee expensive.

Immune Support: Dogs Have Allergies Too!

This may sound ridiculous, but it's true. There has been an alarming rise in dog allergies over the past decade.

For lack of a better term, you'll be chasing your tail if you keep treating recurring allergy symptoms with antihistamines, steroids, special diets. The right treatment is to target immune health and immune health is linked to the gut. Supplements for gut health will help your dog deal with allergies.

The COVID-19 Puppy Crisis

If you are anxious, and find something that will help, wouldn't you want to try it? Dog mental health is an important issue that you may overlook, possibly because you may not even have heard of helping a dog become calmer through supplementation.

Many families adopted puppies during the pandemic lockdown. The change from lockdown to empty homes, as parents return to work and children to school, has been very taxing for many dogs.

You have dogs that have never known anything other than a household that's busy, full of kids that are learning online, and parents who are working from home. They got tons of play time in the backyard and walks because it was the only thing you were allowed to do under government sanctions.

Okay so now we're going back to work, kids are going back to school and these poor dogs are wondering: Where's the playtime? Where are my walks? It is extremely anxiety-inducing for a dog to see the change in the dynamic almost overnight.

Supplementation is something that will help them as they learn the new way of doing things.

It also helps if you just have an anxious dog, anxious because they hate thunderstorms, they hate car rides or they hate when the UPS guy drives up. Thus, if you've got a dog that is high strung and anxious, and you can find a way to just help take the edge off, why wouldn't you? It'll help them with their long-term health, it'll help them with their training, it'll help with them being happier dogs.

Supplements for Anxiety

- L-Theanine
- S-Adenosylmethionine (SAMe)

These supplements can help dogs be happier.[1] They work to make your dog calmer, help them learn new habits smoothly and deal with stimuli that frighten them.

Your Dog Deserves High Quality Supplements

We're gonna sound like a broken record. Your dog trusts you with its life. You adopted or purchased this animal and are responsible for its quality of life. Your care will make all the difference. Like any member of your family, your dog has specific needs that you can fulfill as a loving dog parent.

While you need to stay away from fad diets, supplements can fill the gaps in your dog's nutrition to make sure they're the healthiest they can be. Supplements are not just a boost of 'extra' health. For many dogs, proper supplementation of nutrients is essential. Once again, do your research!

Key Takeaways:

- Even a very high-quality diet provides just the baseline of your dog's nutritional needs
- Supplements can prevent and control disease, so there's no good reason to miss out on their benefits.
- The three focus areas are
  - Joint care - Oral care - Skincare
- Supplements can also help you support your dog's immune system
- **Don't chase your tail! Supplements can help you cure the root of a problem instead of attempting to fix symptoms in an endless cycle.**

- Don't forget mental health! Supplements can be the difference between a happy dog and a miserable dog. Your dog's mental health can be greatly improved through proper dosing of calming, natural supplements.
- To get the best supplements for your dog, make sure the products are made of high-quality ingredients, are backed by research, and are easy and fun for your dog.

Chapter 5

Husbandry and Grooming: How to Pamper Your Dog

How much grooming does my dog need? How do I take care of its appearance? How often should I bathe my dog? How do I cut down on grooming bills?

To treat your dog with all the love and care it deserves, you have all you need to know in this chapter. A clean, shiny dog reflects its owner's care and commitment. We use the word husbandry for your pet's day to day care, especially when it comes to things like bedding and their coat care.

> "You do not own a dog. You have a dog. And the dog has you."
> Chelsea Handler

infections. Good care routines reduce the risk for injury and discomfort. A comfortable, pampered dog is also a happy dog. It will cut down on your cleaning time too and who doesn't want that?

Grooming is Not Just About Vanity

It'll cut down on vet visits, seriously.

You will not be paying for skin infections, hot spots, or ear infections. Good care routines reduce the risk for injury and discomfort. A comfortable, pampered dog is also a happy dog. Good husbandry will also cut down on your home cleaning time and who doesn't want that?

Coat Care

Beautiful humans have clear skin, and beautiful dogs have shiny coats. Different breeds have different requirements. Your work on getting the right tools, bedding, and diet for your dog will quickly pay off with results in its appearance.

Long-haired dogs

Are you vacuuming so much hair that you can literally knit an entire new dog? It must be driving you nuts, and you know there should be a way to avoid all those grooming fees. One of the most effective ways to reduce shedding is diet.

Diet

Our guidelines in Chapters 1 and 2 will help you choose the right foods for your dog. Don't underestimate the power of a good diet for your dog's coat.

For example, Taryn's family has a husky. Her shedding was ridiculously epic. They were vacuuming, two to three times a day. It was driving them nuts and they didn't feel like going to a groomer and paying $200 a month for her to be groomed.

They had to learn how to properly take care of her coat. Step one was adjusting her diet to help decrease the shedding, making sure that her diet was loaded with healthy fatty acids. It seemed too good to be true, but that made an immediate change. Look at the previous chapter to see if supplements are right for your dog.

The Right Tools

Is your dog's brush right for her coat?

Taryn's wasn't. It wasn't getting her dogs undercoat properly, which was causing her all kinds of discomfort. She talked to the groomer and, yes, spent a small fortune on brushes. Now she has three different brushes because she has three different layers to her coat. Now she gets brushed on a regular basis, and they don't have to vacuum 80 times a day. That is husbandry.

Bedding

It's the same thing for her bedding. Taryn was not going to buy her a big, huge, fluffy bed due to the fact it's just going to hold onto all the hair and thus never being able to get it all out. Now the dog has a mat that they can just take a cloth and wipe down.

It comes back down to knowing your breed, buying something that is specific to your dog's coat and its length, and taking care of their needs appropriately.

Bathing

Frequency

Dogs need to be bathed way less often than a lot of people think. Even once a week is too much for many dogs. A good brush can help your dog look neat. Brush your dog 2-3 times a week. Most dogs only need to be bathed if they're visibly dirty.

Products

Wipes can be a great way to spot clean a dog between washes. However, be wary of alcohol based wipes that can be drying for your dog. For bath products, choose mild shampoos and avoid products with excessive additives and alcohol. Many dogs have sensitive skin. Look for natural, gentle products.

Our Little Secret Trick for Nail Trimming

Click cutting dogs' nails takes forever. Nails can also become an unexpected, but high vet expense!

Part of Taryn's older dog's thyroid condition is that her nails became incredibly brittle. Two times after trimming her nails, they ended up in the vet's office because the nails split right into the bed. The first trip was $500, the second trip was over $800 as she had to be anesthetized, the nail had to be removed, the nail bed had to have antibiotics, you name it, a very, very expensive nail trim.

Since they started using their secret tool, they have never had a problem! Everybody's seen Pretty Paws. It's that little nail grinder that you buy at the pet store. It does a good job but it just takes too long.

They got this idea, and they went and bought a Dremel at Home Depot. They know it may sound crazy but hear them out. They keep it at a low speed with high grit sandpaper.

This Dremel has changed their life.

They can do three dogs, zipping their nails down to the quick without any bleeding, without any worry about cracking their nails at all. It takes maybe 15 minutes to do three dogs, all their nails, and it is dead quiet in the house, no clicking from clipped nails on my tile.

Everybody's paws are nice and happy, and we don't have to pay for emergency vet bills.

Flea Control

Fleas can be very persistent and very annoying to deal with. But we'd never recommend store-bought flea treatments, no matter what claims the company makes. **The dangerous effects of store-bought flea shampoos are:**

Number 1, store bought flea shampoos are never effective. They may kill the fleas present on your dog, but when it steps out, they'll all come back.

Number 2, flea shampoos can have extremely adverse effects on your dog.

Many over-the-counter flea treatments contain insecticides called permethrins that are health hazards for dogs.

Dogs exposed to permethrin can get seizures and neurological damage. The ingredient is also highly toxic to cats, so it's not worth the risk.

No pet store, grocery store, or spa treatment promises to be totally effective and safe for your pet.

What's the solution for fleas?

If your dog has been exposed to fleas, there are two steps to take:

- A diluted solution of Dawn dish soap will get fleas off your dog's coat without stripping its skin too much.
- A trip to the vet is necessary for flea control. Get a prescription treatment for fleas as soon as you can.

Prescription treatments are expensive, but emotionally and financially easier than a vet visit for side-effects of store-bought flea treatments. The expense is part of your efforts to create a safe and healthy life for your dog.

A Word About Breeds

We keep repeating "know your breed" in this book. Before you get a dog, consider getting a mixed breed. They are usually hardier than purebreds. There are also online forums about mixed breeds to help you talk to others with the same kind of dog.

It Takes a Village

For all husbandry considerations, don't be afraid to reach out to people. Research your breed, talk to other people. There are so many online forums for specific breeds of dogs, even for breed mixes. Get online, talk to people, listen to their experience with their dogs, do your research.

Know what you need for your animal and then pay attention to

> "Folk will know how large your soul is, by the way you treat a dog."
> Author, academic and political expert Charles F. Doran

your animal. For instance, if you're noticing that a brush isn't working quite well for your dog, go talk to the groomer. In conclusion, watch your animal. Your animal will tell you when something is not right.

If that happens, you are not alone. You are part of a huge community of dog-owners not just in your neighborhood, but your country and the world. Ask around, involve your vet and groomer, and you can keep your dog happy, healthy, and beautiful.

Key Takeaways:

- Quality grooming will save you hundreds in medical bills for your dog.
- Husbandry includes diet, coat care, nail care, and the curation of your dog's surroundings, like its bedding.
- You do not need a professional groomer all the time. Do your research and buy quality tools.
- Invent your own solutions, like our super quick nail trimming secret!
- Talk to your vet, your groomer, and other dog parents about dog care to learn tips and tricks
- Listen to your dog and watch for any areas that require special care.

Chapter 6

Safety: Protect Your Dog from Hazards You May Overlook

**How do I dog-proof my home?
How do I choose the safest toys?
What are the safety hazards I might miss?**

When people talk about keeping your dog healthy and cutting vet bills in half, they often miss an obvious threat to your dog's well-being: accidents. To ensure the long-term health of your dog, you need to dog-proof your home and your daily habits.

Dog safety is very similar to keeping a home safe for a child. Your dog will grow and change. So will your safety needs. With your dog's breed and age in mind, you can make sure that your house and your dog's toys are safe.

> Before you get a dog, you can't quite imagine what living with one might be like; afterward, you can't imagine living any other way." – Caroline Knapp

Puppy-Proof Your Home

Puppies are curious and will chew on anything. Think like your dog. Look around your home and try to see what will catch its attention. Here is a list of things that may be risky for your dog:

1. Toilet Bowl Cleaner

It's easy to leave cleaner poured in the toilet bowl uncovered. But your dog may decide that it's a water bowl and drink it. The bleach and corrosives can be lethal for a dog. At the very least, it will cause a stressful, expensive trip to the vet who will need to counteract the effects of the bleach. There should be no cleaner left in the bowl, in the toilet brush holder, or an accessible spot in the bathroom.

> "In order to really enjoy a dog, one doesn't merely try to train him to be semi human. The point of it is to open oneself to the possibility of becoming partly a dog."
> – Edward Hoagland

2. Electric Cords and Wires

Sounds straightforward, right? Your bedside or floor lamps, standing fans, laptops, phones, T.V, iron.... all come with cords and wires that puppies love. It's obvious why a dog should not find wires: electric shocks. They're also dangerous for the dog, especially if it swallows a plug or wire. Included is you will also end up with damaged appliances.

3. Bones

Chicken bones or pork chops left on the kitchen counter can quickly become a vet emergency. Especially if they're cooked. Small bones can get stuck in your dog's throat, stomach, or intestines. A small piece can block your dog's windpipe. Hard pieces can break a tooth. Peritonitis is a stubborn bacterial infection caused by bones making holes in your dog's stomach. All these major issues can be prevented with a little care.

4. Fireplaces, grills, hot surfaces

Dogs may reach for charcoal in fireplaces and grills. Keep fireplaces covered, and ovens closed. Never leave open fires, stove-tops unattended. This includes irons, steamers, even hot pans, that may cause a disaster in a curious pet's paws.

5. Just About Anything

If your dog has a special affinity for an object that's not meant for it, keep it out of reach. Dogs can be taught to stay away from certain things. Lots of pretty decorations are dangerous for your dog. Train your dog, and you can worry about a pretty house after your dog learns to be safe.

Take Safety in Your Own Hands

Don't trust the pet store. Many people think that if something is available at the pet store, it's totally safe. That is very far from the truth. Your specific dog's physique and habits will help you make good decisions about toys and collars.

Rope toys are a top hazard for dogs. If your dog chews and destroys toys, rope toys are not the solution. Your dog will swallow the rope and your vet will have to take mounds of rope out.

Collars are not a one-size-fits-all deal. A poorly fitting collar can cause bone issues. Choose a collar that will work with your dog's breed. For example, some breeds are prone to bone issues. If you use just a straight collar your dog is going to end up with disc issues, hip issues, or neck issues. So do your research.

Pinch collars are common but are not good for your dog. They put the dog in pain, and instead of teaching it good behavior, you teach your dog to expect and fear pain.

Harnesses are a much better choice than collars. Still, you need to do your research to buy a breed-specific harness. Harnesses allow your dog to gently learn loose leash walks without pain.

Your Dog vs. The Outdoors

You know what you have in your house and can keep it away from your dog. What about the outdoors?

Again, research is your best friend. Look around your yard and the spaces you share with neighbors, like fences. If you take your dog out to walk in a green area, take note of all the different kinds of plants and trees there.

Many deciduous trees have berries that are very toxic to dogs. A neighbor's hedge could mean a trip to the ER for your dog. Put up fences so your dog does not even sniff a potentially toxic hedge in a neighbor's yard. In your own yard, get rid of plants that could harm your dog. Keep your yard clean so that nothing smaller than three inches is lying around.

At the end of it all, a well-trained dog is a safe dog. A dog who'll listen to you before sniffing something suspicious or drop pork chops from his mouth at your command, will be safe. Make sure you're training your dog well.

How Taryn's all-natural hack became an emergency vet trip.

We talked about how a dog's breed-specific habits and physique dictate safety. This cannot be stressed enough. You could be trying your best, but if you do choose the wrong thing for your dog, you'll end up doing more harm than good. For example, Taryn loved the idea of giving their dogs cow hocks that they get from the butcher.

They boiled them and let the dogs chew them. They loved the idea that they were all-natural and free of preservatives or harmful chemicals.

However, they did not think about how their dog Luna, with her long face and narrow muzzle was at risk because of her head shape. She got her muzzle stuck in a cow hock bone. The vet had to go to a hardware store to buy a saw. It was very hard to watch him cut the bone with the saw, while Luna was sedated. They also had to get treatment for the abrasions caused by the saw.

Things that are great for your friend's dog, or one of your dogs, could be a $1000 vet trip for your other dog. So do your research, look at your dog, know its habits and make informed decisions.

This may sound tedious; an ounce of prevention is certainly worth a pound of cure. It's easy to not leave a plate of pork chops sitting on your kitchen counter. It's just plain better to be aware about what is in your home, rather than to sit in a vet's office explaining why your dog is now pooping pencil in pretty colors.

Key Takeaways:

- Dog-proof your home and yard. Anything smaller than 3 inches is a hazard.
- Do your research about vegetation around your home. Many plants are toxic to dogs.
- Bones, cords, toilet bowl cleaners... adapt your habits to keep these things out of reach.
- Collars and harnesses need to be breed specific to prevent bone issues.
- A well-trained dog is a safe dog.
- Research, research, research. Many safety guidelines are breed specific.

Chapter 7

How to Train Your Dog

How does a dog become a part of the family? How does a dog learn to be at their best behavior? What kind of dog stays out of trouble?

For many, many dog issues, the answer is high quality training.

As a dog lover, you love seeing TikTok videos of pets doing cute tricks. You want your dog to shake a paw, play dead.

However, tricks are just bonuses. Training is integral to the development of your dog into a happy, healthy member of your family, who is safe and well-loved.

> "Discipline isn't about showing a dog who's boss; it's about taking responsibility for a living creature you have brought into your world."
> – Cesar Millan

The Importance of Good Training

Training sets the pattern from day one for your dog's whole life. Here are two very basic but extremely important examples:

You want your dog to come when it's called. Of course, this makes your life easier. Nevertheless, more importantly, it's crucial for your dog's well-being. A well-trained dog, who runs into a street but returns on a single call is less likely to get hit.

Or think about the dog that has the chicken bones in its mouth that somebody accidentally left out on the kitchen counter. When told to drop them, the dog immediately obeys. You know what?

"Even the tiniest poodle or chihuahua is still a wolf at heart."
Dorothy Hinshaw

That's a $3,000 vet bill you save because you don't need to get the bones removed from its stomach.

We cannot emphasize enough: An untrained dog is a miserable dog. Think about yourself as a human being, or your children if you have any. When you don't learn boundaries and rules around good behavior, you are set up to become miserable. You cause discomfort for others around you. In the case of dogs, 'discomfort' can quickly escalate to life-threatening situations.

Your Dog Needs to Know Their Place in the Pack

You and your family are your dog's family. A well-trained dog knows exactly where its place is in the pack. Through training, your dog learns its role and feels good about fulfilling the role.

An untrained dog is miserable because it does not know its place in the pack. We all subconsciously or consciously take on roles in our families and friend groups. When we have a part to play, we draw happiness and satisfaction from succeeding at it.

This is exactly what training teaches a dog. When trained well, your dog learns to keep your family happy. Your dog also learns to trust you, often with its life, and obey you to be able to live its best life.

It's no wonder then, that people spend more time with their dogs, if they're trained well. Your dog will be a source of joy for you, instead of worry or even resentment.

The First Basic Rule
Set boundaries from day one.

It's all too easy to spoil a puppy. If you have children and other family members, make sure everyone is on board with how you want to train your dog. A puppy who's carried around all day by a doting child will form core behaviors because of this treatment. The puppy will learn that she's the top dog of the house who doesn't need to get up to go anywhere. And it will expect to be carried around for its whole life and drive you nuts. This may not be a problem for a toy breed, but with a large dog, it will cause problems.
Especially if you want to train your dog as a work animal.

Know what dynamic you can handle with your dog, its breed, and the role you expect it to take in your family. Set boundaries from day one.

The 'Big Four' of the First Six Months

Here is a secret that will get you ahead of the multitudes of relatively well-trained dogs all over the country. Master these four basic commands in the first six months of your dog's life: stay, sit, leave it, and an excellent recall. Your dog should do all these. Most importantly, it should promptly return to you when you call its name.

These are the 'Big Four' of the first six months. If your dog has a solid grip on these commands, you're on your way to making your dog the charming local or internet center of affection.

What if Your Dog is a Rescue?

First of all, hats off to you if you rescue a pet, especially an older dog. You're an amazing human being.

Not enough people do it. For an older rescue dog, your love, assurance, and persistence can make a great difference.

The Assessment Period

Spend the first week or so just observing your new animal's behavior. Your dog at this point doesn't know you, you don't know it, and thus you have no idea. Sometimes you may know the animal's history. However, shelters often give make-believe backstories to dogs, or give you no information. Spend time observing the dog. Notice any behaviors that you want to change and make notes.

The Assessment Period

Most importantly, note the behaviors that you already like. Don't forget this step, because it is just as, if not more, crucial as the first one. You need to know what to praise the dog for. Pick up on its good behaviors, and make sure to provide encouragement.

This assessment period is so important because you're building trust and you're giving the dog time to adjust to its new situation. Once your dog settles in, you'll have a good idea of where you're at.

Begin training after a week or so of noting positive and negative behaviors. For rescue dogs, love and reassurance needs to be at the forefront of your training. This dog needs to feel a hundred times over, that no matter what happens, it is secure and safe in your home. When you build a bond with love and encouragement, the dog will do anything for you.

Be Mentally Prepared

Dogs that have been surrendered to pounds or to rescue organizations are usually there because they suffered some form of trauma, even if it's just from being abandoned. Understand that from the get-go. Be prepared to be patient. This dog may howl for no apparent reason. It could just be scared or anxious.

If your rescued pet is still a puppy, you may need a firmer hand. An older dog may respond better to more affection than firmness. In both cases, you still need boundaries. However, get down on the floor Be with them, reassure them, make sure that they know that they're safe. A dog who trusts you and feels your love will want to make you happy in any way it can.

What Kind of Training Works Best?

There are so many conflicting philosophies about training dogs out there. It's easy to get confused.

One word of advice? Find a good trainer. A trainer can at least get you started on the right track. Trainers that work with treats to begin with, in my opinion, are not the best. However, click training works. In this kind of training, the end game is that the dog looks at you and wants to make you happy.

This is how you make the dog aware of its place in the pack. You give it a role to fulfill in your life, which will also keep your dog happy.

Fixes For Common Behavioral Issues

You can classify behavioral issues into two categories. You have your typical puppy behavior issues that you need to work on from day one and then you have behavioral issues because you didn't train properly in the beginning.

Puppy issues

Puppy behavioral issues are very easily rooted out if they're dealt with as early as possible. For example, you may have a puppy who tends to chew on inappropriate objects. Redirect the behavior of your puppy: tell him no. Or say no and give it a toy to communicate how some things are

"A well-trained dog will make no attempt to share your lunch. He will just make you feel so guilty that you cannot enjoy it."—Helen Thomson

ok to chew on. There's a lot of different ways that you can overcome those typical puppy behaviors.

Aggression

Now, if you are having other behavioral issues, especially from a shelter animal, it can be much more difficult to deal with. Aggression is common in older, traumatized dogs. They may be violent in situations when they're afraid. A dog may only be aggressive towards other animals, to people, to men, women, children, to name a few.

The best you can do for such a dog is to bring it for professional help. At the very least, a short period of professional training will get the ball rolling in the right direction.

Just because a dog has a behavioral issue doesn't mean it needs to be dumped at a pound. In 25 years of training dogs, we've only come across one dog that was beyond help. And that was because it was from a fight ring. Beyond that, we have tackled the toughest behavioral issues and usually, sadly, it's not the dog's fault, it's the humans.

The dog takes cues from you. Once you figure out what you've done wrong, you can fix that behavior. A dog is never aggressive due to inherent character flaws. The dog loves you. It needs to be told if its behavior isn't ok. The dog will want to change to make you happy.

Separation Anxiety

An anxious dog may act out. If your pet is dealing with changes in routine that cause separation anxiety, you must fix the root of the problem. Help your dog adjust. Slowly break them into the new normal. If you need to start leaving your dog alone for the first time, plan and follow our guide for helping your dog.

Now first, there is something that should not be your first step. We talked about supplementation and medications for anxiety in the last chapter. Introducing anxiety medication out of the blue will not fix everything and can cause issues. If the separation anxiety is very severe, start supplementing with 100% natural solutions. Natural supplements can help the pet feel calmer, more open to training and the change in scheduling.

You may need something a little stronger if things don't go well, and that is where you'd seek the help of your caring, concerned veterinarian. However, focus on easing your dog into learning new routines instead of looking for medical solutions from the get-go.

If you think you need a natural supplement to help your dog, it will help them with the first phase of training. Start leaving them alone for consistently longer periods of time to help them ease into it.

Crate Training vs Free Roaming

Dogs are all different and you need to know your dog. For Jasper, we started with a very large kennel. Although we believe in letting dogs roam free, Jasper was different. He seemed happier to have a dark place to go, rather than roaming over the house as that just seemed to make his anxiety go through the roof. We started with a treat, and his food bowl with just a little bit of kibble, and we'd only leave him for 15 minutes maximum. We would do this a couple times. Then every time we would leave, we make it a little bit longer over time.

This can help your dog get used to spending time without you.

You must remember that your dog is in a groove, and completely changing its schedule out of nowhere, is going to cause issues.

You have to slowly make changes until the pet is comfortable with those changes. It's going to take time. However, if you do it right, then you will see that anxiety come down quite a bit.

Doggy Day-Care

For extended periods of time away, pets can benefit from daycare, boarding facilities, or pet sitters. This can help their separation anxiety and give them a chance to socialize. Daycare and boarding also comes with its own challenges. From choosing the right care, to making sure your dog will adjust and behave well, you'll be thinking about a lot of things in your transition phase.

How to choose a good Daycare and Boarding facility

First, talk to your trusted veterinarian. They usually have a list of people that they trust or know, who they're willing to recommend.

If they're not sure of anybody locally, there's a lot of different companies online like rover.com that allow you to shop for a pet sitter, boarding facility, or doggy daycare. What I like about these is that they show you actual verified reviews. You know how many stars each person got, how many repeat customers they have.

See descriptions of the service to find one that suits you. Some services update you with pictures every two hours. They send pictures of your dog, what it's doing, who it's playing with. That gives you peace of mind knowing that your pet is in an environment where it's getting what it needs.

Red Flags

If they're not asking for a meet and greet and taking a full history of your pets, run as fast and as far as you possibly can. You want somebody that is interested in your pets, and their wellbeing. They should be interested in being a good fit, not just looking for your cash.

When you see reviews, steer clear of those who do not have repeat customers or do not have consistently high ratings. A 'good deal' is not worth the setbacks in training that come with unprofessional sitters. It is imperative. Do your research.

Helping Your Dog Adjust to Socializing

This is one of the areas where the importance of caring professionals becomes very clear. To help your dog adjust to socializing with other dogs in daycare and boarding, you need to make sure a professional is handling them.

Socialization needs to happen in a very controlled environment. If you feel that you're going to be an anxious mess you should not be part of it. Find somebody who is going to be there that is going to be able to control their emotion because the pet will pick up on any negative emotions.

When professionals do meet and greets, they learn about your dog and socialize them accordingly. Often, their policy and way of doing things is to have two dogs that are regular daycare dogs, super laid back, not food aggressive, not toy aggressive. They just are good, well natured, well-trained dogs, and that's who you want to initially introduce your dog to.

If you're taking a reactive dog that has never played with another dog, and you're gonna try and pair it with another reactive dog that has never played with another dog, guess what, you're gonna end up with a vet bill and about 30 stitches. Choose carefully, do it in a controlled environment with professionals. I don't suggest going to your local dog cafe if your dog is not used to being around other animals or other people. If you do, you're turning it into such a traumatic situation that you're setting yourself back very much. It needs to be controlled, one to two dogs that you know are nonreactive, are well trained, and make it a positive experience. Keep it short and sweet at the beginning and grow from there.

Sometimes people think that they can go to the local bookstore and get a book about dog training and then suddenly, they're magically going to know what to do. There's a lot more to it than meets the eye. Working with a trainer, somebody that has years of experience, that has gone to school, that knows what they're doing, one that trains the dog and owner, that is the best gift you can give your dog. We support both private training and group training so that your dog gets socialization, along with any specific needs that need to be addressed one on one. A trained dog that knows its place in the pack in your household is one that makes everybody happy.

Key Takeaways:

- To train a dog well is to set them up for a happy, successful life.
- Set boundaries from day one.
- Bring everyone in the family on board with rules about engaging with your pet.
- Professional training is the best gift you can give your dog.
- The best training taps into your dog's desire to make you happy.
- No dog is beyond help.
- **Your dog loves you. Train it well to help it make both of you happy.**

Chapter 8

Detect Illness: How to Catch Chronic Problems Early

What signs do I need to look out for? Is it regular behavior or a sign of illness? What do I do if my dog has diarrhea? Nausea? Should I be concerned if my dog is overweight? What steps can I take at home before going to the vet?

Our furry friends cannot talk to us to tell us when they're in pain or feel sick. It makes matters harder that dogs are also very good at hiding their symptoms. You'll know, of course, when a dog is puking all over your carpet. But chronic illnesses develop stealthily and shorten your pet's life. You need to be very alert to changes in your dog's body and habits.

> "Dogs are wise. They crawl away into a quiet corner and lick their wounds and do not rejoin the world until they are whole once more." – Agatha Christie

Catching illness early dramatically increases the chances of recovery, or manageable treatment.

Common signs to look for

Is your dog:
- exercising a bit less?
- sleeping more?
- eating less?
- not interacting with the family much?
- losing or gaining weight without an obvious reason?
- Is its coat less shiny?

Those are all very common signs that something is not quite right with your pet. These warning bells mean it's time to get your friend to the vet.

The Senior Profile

We're big proponents of the senior profile. The second your animal turns seven years old, they should have a full blood panel done by your vet. This age could be earlier if you have a dog breed with a shorter life span.

A full blood panel at this age has many benefits. For one, it will immediately show you if your dog has any medical issues. You can catch these issues and nip them in the bud.

A blood panel will also help you assess how much care your dog will need in the coming years. A good Senior Care plan, made in advance, will prepare you.

The test results will also provide you a baseline for the future. In case your dog shows any symptoms in a year or so, these test results will be a reference point for you to compare and learn from. Changes in the blood panel results will reveal the root cause of your dog's illness and help you treat it in time.

It's normal for your dogs to slow down as they age. However, if something feels off or your dog's behavior changes, it's time for a second opinion from your vet.

Normal Behavior or Emergency?

Panting in dogs is a normal behavior that can often tell you if your dog is in pain. If your dog has just finished some hard exercise, panting is normal.

However, if the panting is accompanied by other behaviors, like pacing, and not settling in a comfortable position, your dog could be in pain. Dogs may lift a paw or show you obviously where the pain is, but even if they don't, it could be serious. If none of your soothing tactics, like lying down with your dog, or any other things that worked in the past, isn't working, it's an emergency. It needs to be addressed immediately by a vet.

Forget the adage, if my dog's nose is wet, it's fine. Not true. Things you may ignore, like abnormal panting and discomfort could be a medical emergency.

Common Dog Ailments and What to Do

Diarrhea

Diarrhea is very common. The first steps you can take are:
- **Pull food for at least 6 hours.**
- **Provide ample supply of fresh water**
- **Slowly reintroduce food after 12 hours**
- **Look for symptoms to know if you should go to the vet.**

Do you need to go to the vet if your dog has diarrhea?

It depends. Stress can cause diarrhea. Is your dog prone to stress? Have you changed its routine suddenly? Did you have to be gone an extra hour? Were there firecrackers? Diarrhea from stress usually subsides without the aid of a vet.

Another reason can be food. If you recently changed your dog's food, check the ingredients and keep an eye out for how your dog reacts to different foods.

Your dog may also have eaten something it is not supposed to. Check if any chunks of toys or plants are missing. Check with family members. Someone may confess they hated dinner and slipped some to the dog.

In the above cases, your dog may have a couple bouts of diarrhea, but still have high energy and an appetite. Water and some time without food will be enough.

If there is no obvious cause, look for symptoms that may indicate serious trouble. If there's blood in your dog's feces, if it's straining to defecate, obviously uncomfortable and guarded, you need to call your vet as soon as possible.

Vomiting

This is a bigger concern than diarrhea. Unlike cats, dogs don't vomit a lot. Look at your dog's vomit to see what might be causing it:

- If your dog is throwing up undigested bits of food, then it's probably eating too quickly. This is most likely the case if your pet wolfs down its food, and throws it up 10 minutes later in a warm pile of mush. The solution is to reduce the food you give your dog. Put food in a raised bowl to slow down your dog.

- If your dog is throwing up stomach bile, it has either eaten something it's not supposed to, or is stressed out. If it happens once, and your pet seems happy, there is no cause for concern. You'll need to pull food for a few hours, make sure your pet has lots of water, and keep an eye on them.
- If your dog vomits more than once or twice in half an hour, or you see blood, it's time to call the vet.

Your knowledge of your pet will help you here. You know its usual energy levels and demeanor. Big changes in energy and demeanor indicate that something is off.

Ear infections

Dogs with floppy ears are prone to infections. Those cute floppy ears like to harbor bacteria and keep everything moist and warm in there. Bacteria, and especially yeast love this environment.

Most common ear infections are, believe it or not, not an infection, it's an overgrowth of yeast. Yeast infections in the ears have the following symptoms:

- a pungent, bready smell in their ears
- waxy yellow buildup

These can be treated at home. Try these remedies:

- Over the counter products can help drain the ear of build-up.
- Natural ingredients like Apple Cider Vinegar or Tea Tree Oil can kill the yeast.
- Avoid alcohol based cleaners that can dry out your dog's ear. You may think that's good, but ears that are too dry can become even more prone to infection.

You need to go to the vet if your dog's ear infection is bacterial. Here are some symptoms to look for:

- If your dog's ear is red and swollen.
- The ear feels hot
- Your dog gets aggressive if you try to touch the ear, i.e it's painful
- Your dog's demeanor is significantly more alert or lethargic

No over the counter medication will help with a bacterial infection. You need to go to the vet as soon as possible. The longer you wait, the worse your dog's condition will get.

Preventing Ear Infections

If you have a floppy-eared dog, you need to take special care to prevent ear infections.

- Clean and dry your dog's ears every time they get wet
- Use an ear wash. You'll need to clean your dog's ears with a cotton ball and a good quality ear wash that is alcohol-free. Dry, clean ears don't often get infected.

In case of ear infections, prevention is much easier on you and your dog than a cure.

Urinary Tract Problems

Urinary Tract Infections (UTIs) cannot be treated at home. You may use probiotic supplements for prevention, but only if you know your dog is prone to UTIs. Older female dogs and diabetic dogs are prone to these infections. Similarly, some breeds are prone to urinary tract stones or crystals, like Shih Tzu, Yorkshire Terriers, and Bichon Frise.

Symptoms of a UTI or similar issues include

- frequent urination, or accidents even in a well-trained dog
- your dog is straining to pee
- cloudy, smelly urine
- blood in urine

These issues cannot be ignored. You need to take your pet to the vet immediately if you notice these symptoms. The doctor will do a urinalysis and determine if there is an infection, or if there are crystals and what type. Treatment is prescribed based on these findings.

Your vet can help you plan for treatment and future prevention of urinary tract issues. They can help you determine if supplements are a good idea, and the kinds of diet changes you need to make for your pet's health.

Skin Issues

Does your dog constantly scratch itself? Have you noticed abnormal spots on your dog's skin? These may be signs of infections or allergies.

Some of these issues are very dog specific and

very dog specific and have relatively simple solutions. Some dogs get hot spots on their skin in the summer. The simple solution is to keep their fur clipped short when it's hot. A dog who is prone to skin issues may also need:

- food and supplements rich in fatty acids for healthy skin
- medicated baths
- over the counter products that keep the skin clean and moisturized

Another cause may be allergies. If your dog is extremely itchy and is chewing holes into itself, you need to take them to the vet.

There are vets who specialize in treating allergies. They can help your dog because this is a specific area of expertise. It's very difficult to detect what a dog is allergic to. Change your dog's environment and do a process of elimination to figure out what your dog is allergic to.

Taryn has a pet who is allergic to wool, and they had to remove their wool carpet. They also found that human food can often trigger allergies.

Mild allergies can be treated at home. Sometimes, a vet may suggest steroids if nothing is working. Try to do as much as possible to find out the dog's specific issue before taking this route.

Dental Disease

Dental problems are more common in little breeds with small mouths, for example Chihuahuas. That's why you see those funny pictures of Chihuahuas with no teeth. It's a sad fact, but it's a disadvantage in their breed.

Dental problems can be prevented with robust diet and supplementation. You can also get additives for your dog's water that prevent tatar build-up.

The most important thing though, is the yearly vet visit.

Dogs who are prone to periodontal disease need to get their teeth cleaned every year. Vets also do regular dental exams to make sure you can catch any problems before they become too big.

If your dog has bad breath, please don't think it's normal. Yes, your pet is an animal, but its mouth should not stink. A vet will help you figure out what's wrong, and suggest what to do.

Stiffness and Pain

Your dog may show signs of pain if it has lower energy, or suddenly has mobility issues. You need a vet to figure out the cause of the pain.

If your senior dog, for example, begins to have trouble climbing stairs, a vet will help you figure out what's wrong. Older dogs often develop arthritis, and need supplements and a good senior diet.

When Taryn's dog Luna started having trouble with stairs, the vet helped them find out that she has degenerating discs in her back. This issue has a totally different treatment protocol than a senior dog's arthritis.

If your dog is in pain, a visit to the vet is necessary to figure out the cause. For pain prevention in dog breeds that are prone to joint issues, supplementing with Glucosamine and Chondroitin from an early age is a common and beneficial practice.

Obesity
Under 5
No dog under five years of age should be obese. It is either not getting enough exercise, or is being overfed.

Dogs above 5

Thyroid issues may be an underlying cause. Many dog breeds are prone to hypothyroidism which can cause sudden weight gain. If your dog has gained a lot of weight in under six months, go to the vet to figure out the cause.

If you can't find an underlying cause, you should still keep an eye on your dog's weight. If your dog has been slowly gaining weight over the years, introducing more physical activity, reducing high-calorie treats, and cutting back on calories will be helpful for your dog.

If the weight gain, or weight loss is rapid, you need a vet to help you figure out the underlying issue.

Know Your Breed

Please do your research about common chronic illnesses in your specific dog. Your research will include asking your vet and your dog's breeder about any potential issues

A good relationship with your vet can help you manage chronic illnesses even before symptoms begin to show. For example, knowing that a large dog may have joint problems will help you get food, supplements, bedding and harnesses that will reduce future risk.

Your Dog Can Live Well Beyond Its Life Expectancy

Veterinary care in the last 20-30 years has improved by leaps and bounds. You can extend your animal's life and improve the quality of their life; thus, you can have a healthy, happy pet for a long time. The trick being, **you must get to the vet while there's still time to do something.**

Don't wait around. You are basically waiting for the symptoms to get worse. That can cost your animal its life. Your care in catching early warning signs will pay off. When you nip illnesses in the bud, you prevent miserable, chronic illnesses that can gnaw away at your pet.

Bottom line

If you're in doubt, if your gut tells you something's not right, trust yourself. You know your pet more than anybody else. Trust your gut and see your vet if anything feels off. You may save your pet's life.

Key Takeaways:

- Look out for symptoms because pets try to hide their issues
- Don't wait for symptoms to get worse
- Get regular medical exams, like the Senior Panel to stay on top of any issues
- Some common ailments can be treated at home.
- If your dog shows signs of low energy, pain, or lack of appetite, you need the vet.
- Nipping problems in the bud can prevent chronic illness
- Trust your gut. Get your pet checked if you are concerned

Chapter 9

Trends to Avoid

We're all addicted to cute pet videos on TikTok. It's hard not to be. Beautiful, fluffy dogs are a joy to watch. How do they look so healthy? Is there a secret supplement? A special diet? How do they learn all those tricks?

Anyone can upload a video and claim they're experts for a TikTok video. Not all influencers can guide you about choices for your dog's health. Many dog health trends are at best a waste of time, and at worst harmful for your dog.

Vegetarian Diets

This may be a no-brainer for you: dogs are omnivores. At the very

"Properly trained, a man can be dog's best friend."— Corey Ford least, dogs need meat. It seems like such an obvious fact; however, many so-called experts tout the benefits of a vegetarian diet for dogs. The trend is dangerously popular. There is little scientific evidence backing their claims, but these people still insist on selling their vegan products and persuading people to accept their erroneous views.

A vet who has gone to school for many years, has studied the metabolism of dogs, and knows their nutritional needs, can never be replaced by influencers, or 'experts.' No blogs, no matter how legit they look, and no biased 'scientific' studies can give you the answers. You have a wonderful source of knowledge within your reach: your vet.

Vets recommend omnivorous food for good reasons regarding gut health and nutritional needs. If you see any websites that make persuasive arguments in favor of vegetarian dog diets, ask your vet. Your vet will say no because they have studied animal metabolism and nutrition. They treat many dogs every single day and know what they're doing.

Raw Food Diets

Many vets are on the fence about this one. The safer option is to not give in to the trend. Commercially available, raw meat-based dog food has been found to contain harmful bacteria. Most raw meat has salmonella. This can not only make your dog sick, but also other members of your family.

The American Veterinary Medical Association (AVMA) does not endorse the use of a raw food diet. It's just not worth the risk. We're talking about extreme illness and even death. The benefits of raw food diets also appear to be grossly exaggerated. A study in 2011 found that 60% of raw food diets have significant nutrient imbalances.

Your well-meaning friends and influencers with beautiful dogs are not your best sources of nutritional information. Your vet is there for that.

Use diets approved by the FDA or the regulatory body in your country for the safety of your dog. If you really want to use some raw food as a supplement, do your research about what you're using. Inform and involve your vet.

Human foods

Trends on social media show people feeding hot dogs, and other such food to dogs, just to record the dog's reaction. This can be very harmful for dogs. You never know what may happen when you feed a dog something that wasn't made for them. Even something like salt that your dog may be getting from your chips or popcorn can be extremely harmful for dogs. Here is a list of some other foods that can hurt your dog:

- **Avocados**
- **Fruits like apples, grapes, and raisins**
- **Chocolate**
- **Alcohol**
- **Onions**
- **Garlic**
- **Artificially sweetened foods that contain xylitol**
- **Caffeine**
- **Dairy products**
- **Macadamia nuts**

What about CBD?

We're big fans of CBD for dog anxiety, but you need to be careful.

CBD, cannabidiol is derived from hemp and cannabis. It does not contain THC, the stuff that gets you high. But many low-quality dog supplements have THC in them. THC is toxic for dogs. We often see many dogs with THC toxicity, but it's an issue that can be easily avoided.

The supplements you see popping up on your Instagram ads may end up harming your dog. Always do your research about supplement companies and ask your vet for recommendations.

Not 'Just a Dog'

Dogs are wonderful creatures who are friendly and loyal, and often very strong. It can be easy to overlook that your large Labrador or German Shepherd is totally dependent on you. This applies to smaller dogs too. Your pet is not 'just a dog'. However, any negligence on your part, or your well-intentioned use of a new trend can be harmful for your pet. **The safety of your dog is your responsibility.**

It's most likely that you love your dog like a family member. Don't let a trendy diet or supplement sway you, no matter how appealing or trustworthy your sources look. Always look at large unbiased studies and consult your vet.

Key Takeaways:

- You are responsible for the safety of your pet
- The best policy is to minimize risk. Fad diets could cause more harm than good
- Your vet is your best resource, not the internet
- CBD can be beneficial for dog anxiety, but low-quality formulas could harm your dog
- No fun tricks or trends are worth your dog's health and life

Chapter 10

The Golden Years: Taking Care of Your Aging Dog

How old is old? What changes do I need to make? How do I lengthen my dog's life?

When your dog starts to age, your role in your dog's life changes. Your active, happy dog might start becoming slow. The dog who used to cheer you up now needs you to support them. You become your dog's caregiver, and this is a huge responsibility.

It's now your privilege, the only chance you have to pay back just even a sliver of what your dog has given you over the years of its life.

"Old dogs, like old shoes, are comfortable. They might be a bit out of shape and a little worn around the edges, but they fit well."
– Bonnie Wilcox

How Old is Old in Dog Years?

Your dog's official step into senior age depends on its breed. Small dogs reach senior status at 11. For mid-sized and larger dogs, this age is lower, at 10 and 8 years. For giant breeds, 7-year-old dogs are seniors.

The Urge to Spoil

If you want to spoil your dog, your go-to should not be food. Yes, it's hard to refuse treats for any dog. For a senior dog who has a few years left, it's even harder. It's tempting to think that now that your dog is old, it's ok to feed them their unhealthy favorites unchecked. All of this comes from a good place, but you must think about your dog. Just because it's a senior doesn't mean it can't live beyond its life expectancy with some care.

Bad food choices can cause major GI problems. The best food is what your dog is familiar with because your priority is comfort. If you have been giving your dog a healthy diet with occasional treats for years, their transition to senior status will be smoother. You want your dog to be as happy as possible. A good diet will keep your dog healthy enough to be happy.

What Adjustments Should I Make for a Senior Dog?

You can spoil your senior dog as much as you want when it comes to comfort. An older dog will need several readjustments in its life to be as comfortable as possible.

Orthopedic Beds

Senior dogs begin to develop arthritis and other joint problems. An older pet may also have a problem getting up from a lying position if it sinks into a plush bed.

A good orthopedic bed, most often made of memory foam, will be perfect for ensuring your dog rests well. The memory foam supports their hip and elbow joints to minimize discomfort. It's also necessary for good blood flow and preventing muscle aches. A bed must also keep your dog cool for better sleep.

Grooming Needs

Senior dogs may develop medical issues that affect their cleanliness. Taryn's dog, Lady, has a thyroid condition that causes a very strong odor. They descale her with a special comb every single day for her comfort and to keep the house from smelling.

Dogs may also develop incontinence which can mean you have more bathing to do. And bathing brings its own challenges when your pet is old. Visual problems make them more scared of what's happening around them. Mobility and joint problems may make it harder for them to stand in the bath and get in and out of it.

Don't let these issues stop you from grooming your dog. Cleanliness is not just an aesthetic choice. Brushing your dog's coat can help you identify if there are any suspicious lumps or skin conditions. A clean dog is also healthier and happier.

You may not be ready for the fact that many groomers don't handle senior dogs who have issues. Search far and wide and find a good groomer who wants to work with your pet.

Routines

Your once energetic, social puppy will start to slow down. It might be hard emotionally, for you and the dog. There are many things you can do to help your dog transition to a quieter life. You may need to keep your furry friend away from the bustle of a house with children or other dogs. Taryn's dog Lady has a quiet, gated room where they feed her, and she sleeps most of the day. She knows that all she has to do is come to the gate when she wants to come out and join the family. She comes out, sits with them and when she wants to leave, she goes to her quiet place.

Your dog may also be too weak for activities it used to enjoy. Lady used to love going out camping with the family, and they thought about doing it again for her one last time as she ages. That would make them feel better but would not be fair to Lady. She's blind and would find it stressful. Home is comforting for her because it's very familiar and she knows exactly where to go.

Your own routine will change too with more cleaning, grooming and care work. **Be prepared to spend a lot of time on pet care**. For example, Taryn needs to wash Lady's bed every day.

Supplementation

Supplements for healthy joints, anxiety, and the gut can help manage your dog's chronic conditions. Your vet should always be on board with your decisions for treating illness and supplementation.

Veterinary Care

There is no substitute for a professional's informed care. The senior profile, also discussed in the last chapter, includes a blood panel that can identify illness or health risks. You can discuss medication and supplements for prevention and disease management and make good decisions for your dog's health.

The Golden Years

As your dog ages, it will change. Your relationship with your dog will change. Your furry friend may develop conditions that make it stink. You might have to change its bedding every day. You may need special equipment and lots of medicine. It's ok to acknowledge that it can get overwhelming.

However, **pets' lives are too short, and your life has been enriched by having them.** Always remember this animal has given you years of absolute loyalty and brought so much enjoyment and companionship to your family. Now you get to repay what they have given you, care for these brief golden years.

Key Takeaways:

- The official 'senior' years of a dog can begin anywhere from 7-11 years old
- Continue to feed your dog a healthy, balanced diet
- Your senior dog will need spaces that provide comfort, familiarity, and safety
- Don't skimp on a quality bed, grooming and veterinary care
- It will get tough. Senior dogs aren't often taken care of, and you're doing a great service.
- Always remember all that your dog has done for you. Embrace the privilege of being able to say thank you in their brief last years.

Chapter 11
Saying Goodbye

The toughest part of being a pet owner is saying goodbye. Whether you're a seasoned dog owner, or just thinking about getting a dog, you need information to prepare you for the inevitable. We're so glad you're here at this part of the book if you don't have a dog yet. You need to know everything that entails dog parenthood, so that you make an informed decision.

Our pets bring us so much joy. We know them for a short period of their lives, but they dedicate their whole life to us. In gratitude for their service and love, we owe them some things that only we can take care of.

Our last and most solemn responsibility is to not leave our pet in pain.

> "Once you have had a wonderful dog, a life without one, is a life diminished."
> Author Dean Koontz

This is a very difficult topic to discuss. If you have a senior dog with many health issues, you know how difficult it is. Seeing your pet in pain is hard enough. It may help you to remember that making the end-of-life decision is a power afforded to you because of good medical care. We can't say it makes this stage any easier, but it does help a little. You can take some comfort in the fact that your pet lived a full life, and in their painful years you were able to decide to end the suffering. It will be painful, and in this chapter, we'll help you make the decision and deal with the loss.

How do I know it's time?

This is a difficult decision to make, and you want to be sure you did the right thing. You don't want to part with your dog too early, and you don't want to prolong their suffering.

The Three Main Markers

If these three things persist, despite all your efforts and medical treatment, it may be time to let go:

- your dog is no longer eating
- has lost control of its bowels and bladder
- is panting in obvious discomfort.

Our rule of thumb is to note when a pet starts losing its zest for life. You will know when you see it. Your dog may show the following signs

- it stops interacting with family members
- it becomes very inactive

However, this does not mean that the first sign of the symptoms is time to part with them.

Consult your vet. A blood panel will let you know what you're up against. Some problems are curable, but some are not. **You'll know it's time when you've exhausted all options for treatment and see your dog suffering all the time.**

Taryn's dog Lady has congestive heart failure due to her thyroid condition. They know it's not very treatable. Right now, she seems to enjoy her time with them as a happy dog, but they know that soon, they'll have to make that phone call. She has lived past her life expectancy and has lived a full life. As much as they don't want to part with her, they know they must do the right thing. It will be selfish to keep her with them, with her suffering unnecessarily. They have a responsibility to make the right choice at the right time, for her sake.

What will saying goodbye be like?

The word euthanasia is very difficult to consider when you think about your dog. It may help you a little to know what the process is like.

It's actually a very peaceful process for your pets. The very first thing is that the vet will assess your animal. They will discuss end of life procedures. At this point you'll probably already have a very great relationship with your veterinarian. You'll be able to decide if all medical resources have been exhausted. You and your vet will see if it's the right thing to do at the time.

Once you're sure, you'll most likely be asked to sign some documentation and make decisions as to how you want your pet's remains handled.

The last moments

Then the vet will come in and sedate your pet. This is key to making sure that your pet is as comfortable as possible. Your dog will be completely unaware of what's happening. The sedation, for the most part, starts the process of actual death. Your pet at this point is already critically ill, and the sedation is enough to slow their body systems down to where they're just asleep.

They are not aware of anything else that is going on. Once that sedation has taken full effect, the doctor will administer a second injection to ensure that the heart is completely stopped. However, your pet feels nothing. Your pet's last moments will be peaceful and calm.

I encourage you to take the time to say your goodbyes. Please know you're doing the right thing. And believe me, you can then mourn the loss of your beloved pet.

How do I get through this?

You will always remember your pet. Chances are you already have memories of every single pet you've had since childhood.

With the passage of time, you can enjoy the memories. Say thanks for the time and the joy that they brought to your life.

Give yourself time to heal. Often, we think that rushing out to get another pet will help. We think we should adopt another dog. We think we should reach out to the breeder we got our last dog from. We think we can try to fill the void with another animal. To each their own, but it's often not helpful. Each pet has their own individuality, their different personalities, so in our experience, rushing into adopting again is not a good idea.

You need time to mourn. You need time to just let yourself heal. Give yourself the space to do that and within a couple months' time, if you still feel strongly that you want to have another pet in your home, start that journey again. However, please give yourself time to grieve.

To be totally honest, you'll never be able to look at pictures of your late dog and not feel a twinge of pain. Taryn knows that there are times when she walks into her living room, she envisions their last dog running around people's ankles, even after months and years have gone by.

End of Life Parties

Many people have a farewell party on one of their dog's last days. It can be a good chance for you to begin processing your grief and get a chance to say goodbye.

Just make sure your dog is comfortable. An animal in a critical condition may not appreciate large gatherings and noise. You'll always cherish the intimate moments with your furry friend, as you make it comfortable and talk to it. You could get paw prints made if your dog is comfortable. DIYing the process of making a paw print can involve your family. You can support each other and make something you'll all be part of.

"A dog has one aim in life... to bestow his heart." Writer and editor J.R. Ackerley

Funerals and Memorials

A celebration of your dog's life could be a beautiful space for the healing you need. It's no different than having a memorial service for a human. It's a part of the grieving process.

A funeral is a space for getting support from your dearest ones. It can give you a sense of closure, and the ritual could provide a small bit of much needed comfort.

Again, your dog spent its whole life in your service, in complete love and adoration for you. All your dog wanted was to make you happy. At the end of their life, you fulfilled the last responsibility you had towards your dog. You did the right thing for them, and you will always be grateful for your dog's love.

Key Takeaways:

- The end-of-life decision is our last and most solemn responsibility. We owe our dogs a peaceful goodbye that ends their suffering.
- There are three main markers that it's time to part with your dog
    - your dog is no longer eating
    - has lost control of its bowels and bladder
    - is panting in obvious discomfort
- Exhaust all medical options to treat the above problems before making a decision.
- Your dog's last moments will be peaceful.
- You'll need to give yourself time and rituals for grieving.

Chapter 12

Some Final Notes

This book is always here to help you. From start to end, you have seen how we covered each stage of your furry friend's life. We equip you with the information, tips, and tricks you need to give your dog its best life. All the advice in this book is not meant to replace the expert opinion of a vet. You now know what questions to ask your vet, and where to involve them.

The Joys of Dog Parenthood

We acknowledged the weight of your responsibilities in this book. Let's not forget how everything you do for your pets is nothing compared to the joy, love, and companionship your dog will give you. It's hard to believe we deserve

> "Dogs are not our whole life, but they make our lives whole."
> Roger A. Caras

dogs. All a dog wants is to make you happy. All the things you need to do for your dog are there to help your dog reach that goal. Good training, safety, healthy diets, and care will help your dog be the best companion to you and your family.

The Importance of Veterinary Care

No advice from influencers, internet experts, friends, or even this book can replace the role of your vet. Whether it's nutritional advice, regular blood panels, catching strange symptoms of illness, or treating illness, your vet should always have the last word.

If you're unsure about something, instead of turning to other people, get a second opinion from another vet. This book is there to help you cut your vet bills, but not to cut your vet out of your life.

Your vet will thank you for taking good care of your pet, so they don't have to use a saw to cut a cow hock off from around your dog's face. Save your vet the hassle of having to treat your dog for preventable issues and know that their help is invaluable for making decisions about how to care for your dog and extend its life.

If you don't have a dog yet

If you're here to decide about adopting a pet, we're so happy you read this book. Especially in the previous chapter, we give you a full picture that shows you the sheer weight, as well as the joy of your responsibility.

We covered all the adjustments you need to make in your home, your behavior, and your family's habits to give a dog a safe and happy environment.

Think about your decision. If you're going out there to find a companion, to add someone to your life, to get a new family member, then you're ready. Yes, dogs are animals. But they're sentient in the sense that sentient creatures are aware of their feelings and emotions. Their lives matter to them, and they have the capacity to feel joy and pleasure, as well as pain and suffering. Be sure that your family, your heart, and your lifestyle have enough room to care for them properly. A dog's life and death are in your hands, and your hard work and deliberation will determine the quality of their lives, and even the quality of their last moments.

A dog changes your life and makes it so much better. Cherish your pet. You can always turn to this book as a companion to make the best decisions for your dog.

Let's give our lovely companions their best lives!

Notes

Chapter 1

Westgarth, Carri, Robert M. Christley, Christopher Jewell, Alexander J. German, Lynne M. Boddy, and Hayley E. Christian. 2019. "Dog Owners Are More Likely to Meet Physical Activity Guidelines than People without a Dog: An Investigation of the Association between Dog Ownership and Physical Activity Levels in a UK Community." Scientific Reports 9 (1). https://doi.org/10.1038/s41598-019-41254-6.

Guéguen, Nicolas, and Serge Ciccotti. 2008. "Domestic Dogs as Facilitators in Social Interaction: An Evaluation of Helping and Courtship Behaviors." Anthrozoös 21 (4): 339–49. https://doi.org/10.2752/175303708x371564.

Chapter 2

"Is Gluten-Free Dog Food Better?" n.d. Www.petmd.com. https://www.petmd.com/blogs/nutritionnuggets/jcoates/2012/nov/is_gluten_free_dog_food_better-29456.

Wall, Tim. "US$7 Million Fine for Mislabeled Pet Food Ingredient Providers." www.petfoodindustry.com, October 17, 2018. https://www.petfoodindustry.com/articles/7572-us7-million-fine-for-mislabeled-pet-food-ingredient-providers?v=preview..

Chapter 3

"An Active Dog Is a Happy Dog | Release the Hounds." Release the Hounds, November 29, 2013. https://www.releasethehounds.ca/a-tired-dog-is-a-happy-dog-by-sarah-pennington/.

Buzzhardt, Lynn. "Agility for Dogs." VCA Animal Hospitals, n.d. https://vcacanada.com/know-your-pet/agility-for-dogs.

Duranton, C., and A. Horowitz. 2019. "Let Me Sniff! Nosework Induces Positive Judgment Bias in Pet Dogs." Applied Animal Behaviour Science 211 (February): 61–66. https://doi.org/10.1016/j.applanim.2018.12.009.

Llera, Ryan, and Lynn Buzzhardt. n.d. "Why Dogs Sniff Rear

Ends." VCA Animal Hospitals. Accessed January 20, 2022. https://vcacanada.com/know-your-pet/why-dogs-sniff-butts.

Chapter 4

Coates, Jennifer. n.d. "Can You Treat Dog Anxiety with OTC Supplements and Calming Products?" Www.petmd.com. Accessed January 20, 2022. https://www.petmd.com/dog/care/can-you-treat-dog-anxiety-otc-supplements-and-calming-products.

Chapter 9

Dodd, Sarah A. S., Jennifer L. Adolphe, and Adronie Verbrugghe. 2018. "Plant-Based Diets for Dogs." Journal of the American Veterinary Medical Association 253 (11): 1425–32. https://doi.org/10.2460/javma.253.11.1425.

Downing, Robert. n.d. "Dogs and Raw Food Diets | VCA Animal Hospitals." Vcahospitals.com. Accessed January 20, 2022. https://vcahospitals.com/know-your-pet/dogs-and-raw-food-diets..

Dillitzer, Natalie, Nicola Becker, and Ellen Kienzle. 2011. "Intake of Minerals, Trace Elements and Vitamins in Bone and Raw Food Rations in Adult Dogs." British Journal of Nutrition 106 (S1): S53–56. https://doi.org/10.1017/s0007114511002765.

www.ingramcontent.com/pod-product-compliance
Lightning Source LLC
Chambersburg PA
CBHW081709100526
44590CB00022B/3708